First State of the Union Address

JAMES BUCHANAN

Published in 1857

TABLE OF CONTENTS

FIRST STATE OF THE UNION ADDRESS

Fellow-Citizens of the Senate and House of Representatives:

In obedience to the command of the Constitution, it has now become my duty "to give to Congress information of the state of the Union and recommend to their consideration such measures" as I judge to be "necessary and expedient."

But first and above all, our thanks are due to Almighty God for the numerous benefits which He has bestowed upon this people, and our united prayers ought to ascend to Him that He would continue to bless our great Republic in time to come as He has blessed it in time past. Since the adjournment of the last Congress our constituents have enjoyed an unusual degree of health. The earth has yielded her fruits abundantly and has bountifully rewarded the toil of the husbandman. Our great staples have commanded high prices, and up till within a brief period our manufacturing, mineral, and mechanical occupations have largely partaken of the general prosperity. We have possessed all the elements of material wealth in rich abundance, and yet, notwithstanding all these advantages, our country in its monetary interests is at the present moment in a deplorable condition. In the midst of unsurpassed plenty in all the productions of agriculture and in all the elements of national wealth, we find our manufactures suspended, our public works retarded, our private enterprises of different kinds abandoned, and thousands of useful laborers thrown out of employment and reduced to want. The revenue of the Government, which is chiefly derived from duties on imports from abroad, has been greatly reduced, whilst the appropriations made by Congress at its last session for the current fiscal year are very large in amount.

Under these circumstances a loan may be required before the close of your present session; but this, although deeply to be regretted, would prove to be only a slight misfortune when compared with the suffering and distress prevailing among the people. With this the Government can not fail deeply to sympathize, though it may be without the power to extend relief.

It is our duty to inquire what has produced such unfortunate results and whether their recurrence can be prevented. In all former revulsions the blame might have been fairly attributed to a variety of cooperating causes, but not so upon the present occasion. It is apparent that our existing misfortunes have proceeded solely from our extravagant and vicious system of paper currency and bank credits, exciting the people to wild speculations and gambling in stocks. These revulsions must continue to recur at successive intervals so long as the amount of the paper currency and bank loans and discounts of the country shall be left to the discretion of 1,400 irresponsible banking institutions, which from the very law of their nature will consult the interest of their stockholders rather than the public welfare.

The framers of the Constitution, when they gave to Congress the power "to coin money and to regulate the value thereof" and prohibited the States from coining money, emitting bills of credit, or making anything but gold and silver coin a tender in payment of debts, supposed they had protected the people against the evils of an excessive and irredeemable paper currency. They are not responsible for the existing anomaly that a Government endowed with the sovereign attribute of coining money and regulating the value thereof should have no power to prevent others from driving this coin out of the country and filling up the channels of circulation with paper which does not represent gold and silver.

It is one of the highest and most responsible duties of Government to insure to the people a sound circulating medium, the amount of which ought to be adapted with the utmost possible wisdom and skill to the wants of internal trade and foreign exchanges. If this be either greatly above or greatly below the proper standard, the marketable value of every man's property is increased or diminished in the same proportion, and injustice to individuals as well as incalculable evils to the community are the consequence.

Unfortunately, under the construction of the Federal Constitution which has now prevailed too long to be changed this important and delicate duty has been dissevered from the coining power and virtually transferred to more than 1,400 State banks acting independently of each other and regulating their paper issues almost exclusively by a regard to the present interest of their stockholders. Exercising the sovereign power of providing a paper currency instead of coin for the country, the first duty which these banks owe to the public is to keep in their vaults a sufficient amount of gold and silver to insure the convertibility of their notes into coin at all times and under all circumstances. No bank ought ever to be chartered without such restrictions on its business as to secure this result. All other restrictions are comparatively vain. This is the only true touchstone, the only efficient regulator of a paper currency-the only one which can guard the public against overissues and bank suspensions. As a collateral and eventual security, it is doubtless wise, and in all cases ought to be required, that banks shall hold an amount of United States or State securities equal to their notes in circulation and pledged for their redemption. This, however, furnishes no adequate security against overissue. On the contrary, it may be perverted to inflate the currency. Indeed, it is possible by this means to convert all the debts of the United States and State Governments into bank notes, without reference to the specie required to redeem them. However valuable these securities may be in themselves, they can not be converted into gold and silver at the moment of pressure, as our experience teaches, in sufficient time to prevent bank suspensions and the depreciation of bank notes. In England, which is to a considerable extent a paper-money country, though vastly behind our own in this respect, it was deemed advisable, anterior to the act of Parliament of 1844, which wisely separated the issue of notes from the banking department, for the Bank of England always to keep on hand gold and silver equal to one-third of its combined circulation and deposits. If this proportion was no more than sufficient to secure the convertibility of its notes with the whole of Great Britain and to some extent the continent of Europe as a field for its circulation, rendering it almost impossible that a sudden and immediate run to a dangerous amount should be made upon it, the same proportion would certainly be insufficient under our banking system. Each of our 1,400 banks has but a limited circumference for its circulation, and in the course of a very few days the depositors and note holders might demand from such a bank a sufficient amount in specie to compel it to suspend, even although it had coin in its vaults equal to one-third of its immediate liabilities. And yet I am not aware, with the exception of the banks of Louisiana, that any State bank throughout the Union has been required by its charter to keep this or any other proportion of gold and silver compared with the amount of its combined circulation and deposits. What has been the consequence? In a recent report made by the Treasury Department on the condition of the banks throughout the different States, according to returns dated nearest to January, 1857, the aggregate amount of actual specie in their vaults is $58,349,838, of their circulation $214,778,822, and of their deposits $230,351,352. Thus it appears that these banks in the aggregate have considerably less than one dollar in seven of gold and silver compared with their circulation and deposits. It was palpable, therefore, that the very first pressure must drive them to suspension and deprive the people of a convertible currency, with all its disastrous consequences. It is truly wonderful that they should have so long continued to preserve their credit when a demand for the payment of one-seventh of their immediate liabilities would have driven them into insolvency. And this is the condition of the banks, notwithstanding that four hundred millions of gold from California have flowed in upon us within the last eight years, and the tide still continues to flow. Indeed, such has been the extravagance of bank credits that the banks now hold a considerably less amount of specie, either in proportion to their capital or to their circulation and deposits combined, than they did before the discovery of gold in California. Whilst in the year 1848 their specie in proportion to their capital was more than equal to one dollar for four and a half, in 1857 it does not amount to one dollar for every six dollars and thirty-three cents of their capital. In the year 1848 the specie was equal within a very small fraction to one dollar in five of their circulation and deposits; in 1857 it is not equal to one dollar in seven and a half of their circulation and deposits.

From this statement it is easy to account for our financial history for the last forty years. It has been a history of extravagant expansions in the business of the country, followed by ruinous contractions. At successive intervals the best and most enterprising men have been tempted to their ruin by excessive bank loans of mere paper credit, exciting them to extravagant importations of foreign goods, wild speculations, and ruinous and demoralizing stock gambling. When the crisis arrives, as arrive it must, the banks can extend no relief to the people. In a vain struggle to redeem their liabilities in specie they are compelled to contract their loans and their issues, and at last, in the hour of distress, when their assistance is most needed, they and their debtors together sink into insolvency.

It is this paper system of extravagant expansion, raising the nominal price of every article far beyond its real value when compared with the cost of similar articles in countries whose circulation is wisely regulated, which has prevented us from competing in our own markets with foreign manufacturers, has produced extravagant importations, and has counteracted the effect of the large incidental protection afforded to our domestic manufactures by the present revenue tariff. But for this the branches of our manufactures composed of raw materials, the production of our own country-such as cotton, iron, and woolen fabrics-would not only have acquired almost exclusive possession of the home market, but would have created for themselves a foreign market throughout the world.

Deplorable, however, as may be our present financial condition, we may yet indulge in bright hopes for the future. No other nation has ever existed which could have endured such violent expansions and contractions of paper credits without lasting injury; yet the buoyancy of youth, the energies of our population, and the spirit which never quails before difficulties will enable us soon to recover from our present financial embarrassments, and may even occasion us speedily to forget the lesson which they have taught. In the meantime it is the duty of the Government, by all proper means within its power, to aid in alleviating the sufferings of the people occasioned by the suspension of the banks and to provide against a recurrence of the same calamity. Unfortunately, in either aspect of the ease it can do but little. Thanks to the independent treasury, the Government has not suspended payment, as it was compelled to do by the failure of the banks in 1837. It will continue to discharge its liabilities to the people in gold and silver. Its disbursements in coin will pass into circulation and materially assist in restoring a sound currency. From its high credit, should we be compelled to make a temporary loan, it can be effected on advantageous terms. This, however, shall if possible be avoided, but if not, then the amount shall be limited to the lowest practicable sum.

I have therefore determined that whilst no useful Government works already in progress shall be suspended, new works not already commenced will be postponed if this can be done without injury to the country. Those necessary for its defense shall proceed as though there had been no crisis in our monetary affairs.

But the Federal Government can not do much to provide against a recurrence of existing evils. Even if insurmountable constitutional objections did not exist against the creation of a national bank, this would furnish no adequate preventive security. The history of the last Bank of the United States abundantly proves the truth of this assertion. Such a bank could not, if it would, regulate the issues and credits of 1,400 State banks in such a manner as to prevent the ruinous expansions and contractions in our currency which afflicted the country throughout the existence of the late bank, or secure us against future suspensions. In 1825 an effort was made by the Bank of England to curtail the issues of the country banks under the most favorable circumstances. The paper currency had been expanded to a ruinous extent, and the bank put forth all its power to contract it in order to reduce prices and restore the equilibrium of the foreign exchanges. It accordingly commenced a system of curtailment of its loans and issues, in the vain hope that the joint stock and private banks of the Kingdom would be compelled to follow its example. It found, however, that as it contracted they expanded, and at the end of the process, to employ the language of a very high official authority, "whatever reduction of the paper circulation was effected by the Bank of England (in 1825) was more than made up by the issues of the country banks."

But a bank of the United States would not, if it could, restrain the issues and loans of the State banks, because its duty as a regulator of the currency must often be in direct conflict with the immediate interest of its stockholders. if we expect one agent to restrain or control another, their interests must, at least in some degree, be antagonistic. But the directors of a bank of the United States would feel the same interest and the same inclination with the directors of the State banks to expand the currency, to accommodate their favorites and friends with loans, and to declare large dividends. Such has been our experience in regard to the last bank.

After all, we must mainly rely upon the patriotism and wisdom of the States for the prevention and redress of the evil. If they will afford us a real specie basis for our paper circulation by increasing the denomination of bank notes, first to twenty and afterwards to fifty dollars; if they will require that the banks shall at all times keep on hand at least one dollar of gold and silver for every three dollars of their circulation and deposits, and if they will provide by a self-executing enactment, which nothing can arrest, that the moment they suspend they shall go into liquidation, I believe that such provisions, with a weekly publication by each bank of a statement of its condition, would go far to secure us against future suspensions of specie payments.

Congress, in my opinion, possess the power to pass a uniform bankrupt law applicable to all banking institutions throughout the United States, and I strongly recommend its exercise. This would make it the irreversible organic law of each bank's existence that a suspension of specie payments shall produce its civil death. The instinct of self-preservation would then compel it to perform its duties in such a manner as to escape the penalty and preserve its life.

The existence of banks and the circulation of bank paper are so identified with the habits of our people that they can not at this day be suddenly abolished without much immediate injury to the country. If we could confine them to their appropriate sphere and prevent them from administering to the spirit of wild and reckless speculation by extravagant loans and issues, they might be continued with advantage to the public.

But this I say, after long and much reflection: If experience shall prove it to be impossible to enjoy the facilities which well-regulated banks might afford without at the same time suffering the calamities which the excesses of the banks have hitherto inflicted upon the country, it would then be far the lesser evil to deprive them altogether of the power to issue a paper currency and confine them to the functions of banks of deposit and discount.

Our relations with foreign governments are upon the whole in a satisfactory condition.

The diplomatic difficulties which existed between the Government of the United States and that of Great Britain at the adjournment of the last Congress have been happily terminated by the appointment of a British minister to this country, who has been cordially received. Whilst it is greatly to the interest, as I am convinced it is the sincere desire, of the

Governments and people of the two countries to be on terms of intimate friendship with each other, it has been our misfortune almost always to have had some irritating, if not dangerous, outstanding question with Great Britain.

Since the origin of the Government we have been employed in negotiating treaties with that power, and afterwards in discussing their true intent and meaning. In this respect the convention of April 19, 1850, commonly called the Clayton and Bulwer treaty, has been the most unfortunate of all, because the two Governments place directly opposite and contradictory constructions upon its first and most important article. Whilst in the United States we believed that this treaty would place both powers upon an exact equality by the stipulation that neither will ever "occupy, or fortify, or colonize, or assume, or exercise any dominion" over any part of Central America, it is contended by the British Government that the true construction of this language has left them in the rightful possession of all that portion of Central America which was in their occupancy at the date of the treaty; in fact, that the treaty is a virtual recognition on the part of the United States of the right of Great Britain, either as owner or protector, to the whole extensive coast of Central America, sweeping round from the Rio Hondo to the port and harbor of San Juan de Nicaragua, together with the adjacent Bay Islands, except the comparatively small portion of this between the Sarstoon and Cape Honduras. According to their construction, the treaty does no more than simply prohibit them from extending their possessions in Central America beyond the present limits. It is not too much to assert that if in the United States the treaty had been considered susceptible of such a construction it never would have been negotiated under the authority of the President, nor would it have received the approbation of the Senate. The universal conviction in the United States was that when our Government consented to violate its traditional and time-honored policy and to stipulate with a foreign government never to occupy or acquire territory in the Central American portion of our own continent, the consideration for this sacrifice was that Great Britain should, in this respect at least, be placed in the same position with ourselves. Whilst we have no right to doubt the sincerity of the British Government in their construction of the treaty, it is at the same time my deliberate conviction that this construction is in opposition both to its letter and its spirit.

Under the late Administration negotiations were instituted between the two Governments for the purpose, if possible, of removing these difficulties, and a treaty having this laudable object in view was signed at London on the 17th October, 1856, and was submitted by the President to the Senate on the following 10th of December. Whether this treaty, either in its original or amended form, would have accomplished the object intended without giving birth to new and embarrassing complications between the two Governments, may perhaps be well questioned. Certain it is, however, it was rendered much less objectionable by the different amendments made to it by the Senate. The treaty as amended was ratified by me on the 12th March, 1857, and was transmitted to London for ratification by the British Government. That Government expressed its willingness to concur in all the amendments made by the Senate with the single exception of the clause relating to Ruatan and the other islands in the Bay of Honduras. The article in the original treaty as submitted to the Senate, after reciting that these islands and their inhabitants "having been, by a convention bearing date the 27th day of August, 1856, between Her Britannic Majesty and the Republic of Honduras, constituted and declared a free territory under the sovereignty of the said Republic of Honduras," stipulated that "the two contracting parties do hereby mutually engage to recognize and respect in all future time the independence and rights of the said free territory as a part of the Republic of Honduras."

Upon an examination of this convention between Great Britain and Honduras of the 27th August, 1856, it was found that whilst declaring the Bay Islands to be "a free territory under the sovereignty of the Republic of Honduras" it deprived that Republic of rights without which its sovereignty over them could scarcely be said to exist. It divided them from the remainder of Honduras and gave to their inhabitants a separate government of their own, with legislative, executive, and judicial officers elected by themselves. It deprived the Government of Honduras of the taxing power in every form and exempted the people of the islands from the performance of military duty except for their own exclusive defense. It also prohibited that Republic from erecting fortifications upon them for their protection, thus leaving them open to invasion from any quarter; and, finally, it provided "that slavery shall not at any time hereafter be permitted to exist therein."

Had Honduras ratified this convention, she would have ratified the establishment of a state substantially independent within her own limits, and a state at all times subject to British influence and control. Moreover, had the United States ratified the treaty with Great Britain in its original form, we should have been bound "to recognize and respect in all future time" these stipulations to the prejudice of Honduras. Being in direct opposition to the spirit and meaning of the Clayton and Bulwer treaty as understood in the United States, the Senate rejected the entire clause, and substituted in its stead a simple recognition of the sovereign right of Honduras to these islands in the following language: The two contracting parties do hereby mutually engage to recognize and respect the islands of Ruatan, Bonaco, Utila, Barbaretta, Helena, and Moral, situate in the Bay of Honduras and off the coast of the Republic of Honduras, as under the sovereignty and as part of the said Republic of Honduras.

Great Britain rejected this amendment, assigning as the only reason that the ratifications of the convention of the 27th August, 1856, between her and Honduras had not been "exchanged, owing to the hesitation of that Government." Had this been done, it is stated that "Her Majesty's Government would have had little difficulty in agreeing to the modification proposed by the Senate, which then would have had in effect the same signification as the original wording." Whether this would have been the effect, whether the mere circumstance of the exchange of the ratifications of the British convention with Honduras prior in point of time to the ratification of our treaty with Great Britain would "in effect" have had "the same signification as the original wording," and thus have nullified the amendment of the Senate, may well be doubted. It is, perhaps, fortunate that the question has never arisen.

The British Government, immediately after rejecting the treaty as amended, proposed to enter into a new treaty with the United States, similar in all respects to the treaty which they had just refused to ratify, if the United States would consent to add to the Senate's clear and unqualified recognition of the sovereignty of Honduras over the Bay Islands the following conditional stipulation: Whenever and so soon as the Republic of Honduras shall have concluded and ratified a treaty with Great Britain by which Great Britain shall have ceded and the Republic of Honduras shall have accepted the said islands, subject to the provisions and conditions contained in such treaty.

This proposition was, of course, rejected. After the Senate had refused to recognize the British convention with Honduras of the 27th August, 1856, with full knowledge of its contents, it was impossible for me, necessarily ignorant of "the provisions and conditions" which might be contained in a future convention between the same parties, to sanction them in advance.

The fact is that when two nations like Great Britain and the United States, mutually desirous, as they are, and I trust ever may be, of maintaining the most friendly relations with each other, have unfortunately concluded a treaty which they understand in senses directly opposite, the wisest course is to abrogate such a treaty by mutual consent and to commence anew. Had this been done promptly, all difficulties in Central America would most probably ere this have been adjusted to the satisfaction of both parties. The time spent in discussing the meaning of the Clayton and Bulwer treaty would have been devoted to this praiseworthy purpose, and the task would have been the more easily accomplished because the interest of the two countries in Central America is identical, being confined to securing safe transits over all the routes across the Isthmus.

Whilst entertaining these sentiments, I shall, nevertheless, not refuse to contribute to any reasonable adjustment of the Central American questions which is not practically inconsistent with the American interpretation of the treaty. Overtures for this purpose have been recently made by the British Government in a friendly spirit, which I cordially reciprocate, but whether this renewed effort will result in success I am not yet prepared to express an opinion. A brief period will determine.

With France our ancient relations of friendship still continue to exist. The French Government have in several recent instances, which need not be enumerated, evinced a spirit of good will and kindness toward our country, which I heartily reciprocate. It is, notwithstanding, much to be regretted that two nations whose productions are of such a character as to invite the most extensive exchanges and freest commercial intercourse should continue to enforce ancient and obsolete restrictions of trade against each other. Our commercial treaty with France is in this respect an exception from our treaties with all other commercial nations. It jealously levies discriminating duties both on tonnage and on articles the growth, produce, or manufacture of the one country when arriving in vessels belonging to the other.

More than forty years ago, on the 3d March, 1815, Congress passed an act offering to all nations to admit their vessels laden with their national productions into the ports of the United States upon the same terms with our own vessels provided they would reciprocate to us similar advantages. This act confined the reciprocity to the productions of the respective foreign nations who might enter into the proposed arrangement with the United States. The act of May 24, 1828, removed this restriction and offered a similar reciprocity to all such vessels without reference to the origin of their cargoes. Upon these principles our commercial treaties and arrangements have been rounded, except with France, and let us hope that this exception may not long exist.

Our relations with Russia remain, as they have ever been, on the most friendly footing. The present Emperor, as well as his predecessors, have never failed when the occasion offered to manifest their good will to our country, and their friendship has always been highly appreciated by the Government and people of the United States.

With all other European Governments, except that of Spain, our relations are as peaceful as we could desire. I regret to say that no progress whatever has been made since the adjournment of Congress toward the settlement of any of the numerous claims of our citizens against the Spanish Government. Besides, the outrage committed on our flag by the Spanish war frigate Ferrolana on the high seas off the coast of Cuba in March, 1855, by firing into the American mail steamer El Dorado and detaining and searching her, remains unacknowledged and unredressed. The general tone and temper of the Spanish Government toward that of the United States are much to be regretted. Our present envoy extraordinary and minister plenipotentiary to Madrid has asked to be recalled, and it is my purpose to send out a new minister to Spain with special instructions on all questions pending between the two Governments, and with a determination to have them speedily and amicably adjusted if this be possible. In the meantime, whenever our minister urges the just claims of our citizens on the notice of the Spanish Government he is met with the objection that Congress has never made the appropriation recommended by President Polk in his annual message of December, 1847, "to be paid to the Spanish Government for the purpose of distribution among the claimants in the Amistad case." A similar recommendation was made by my immediate predecessor in his message of December, 1853, and entirely concurring with both in the opinion that this indemnity is justly due under the treaty with Spain of the 27th of October, 1795, I earnestly recommend such an appropriation to the favorable consideration of Congress.

A treaty of friendship and commerce was concluded at Constantinople on the 13th December, 1856, between the United States and Persia, the ratifications of which were exchanged at Constantinople on the 13th June, 1857, and the treaty was proclaimed by the President on the 18th August, 1857. This treaty, it is believed, will prove beneficial to American commerce. The Shah has manifested an earnest disposition to cultivate friendly relations with our country, and has expressed a strong wish that we should be represented at Teheran by a minister plenipotentiary; and I recommend that an appropriation be made for this purpose.

Recent occurrences in China have been unfavorable to a revision of the treaty with that Empire of the 3d July, 1844, with a view to the security and extension of our commerce. The twenty-fourth article of this treaty stipulated for a revision of it in case experience should prove this to be requisite, "in which case the two Governments will, at the expiration of twelve years from the date of said convention, treat amicably concerning the same by means of suitable persons appointed to conduct such negotiations." These twelve years expired on the 3d July, 1856, but long before that period it was ascertained that important changes in the treaty were necessary, and several fruitless attempts were made by the commissioner of the United States to effect these changes. Another effort was about to be made for the same purpose by our commissioner in conjunction with the ministers of England and France, but this was suspended by the occurrence of hostilities in the Canton River between Great Britain and the Chinese Empire. These hostilities have necessarily interrupted the trade of all nations with Canton, which is now in a state of blockade, and have occasioned a serious loss of life and property. Meanwhile the insurrection within the Empire against the existing imperial dynasty still continues, and it is difficult to anticipate what will be the result. Under these circumstances I have deemed it advisable to appoint a distinguished citizen of Pennsylvania envoy extraordinary and minister plenipotentiary to proceed to China and to avail himself of any opportunities which may offer to effect changes in the existing treaty favorable to American commerce. He left the United States for the place of his destination in July last in the war steamer Minnesota. Special ministers to China have also been appointed by the Governments of Great Britain and France.

Whilst our minister has been instructed to occupy a neutral position in reference to the existing hostilities at Canton, he will cordially cooperate with the British and French ministers in all peaceful measures to secure by treaty stipulations those just concessions to commerce which the nations of the world have a right to expect and which China can not long be permitted to withhold. From assurances received I entertain no doubt that the three ministers will act in harmonious concert to obtain similar commercial treaties for each of the powers they represent.

We can not fail to feel a deep interest in all that concerns the welfare of the independent Republics on our own continent, as well as of the Empire of Brazil.

Our difficulties with New Granada, which a short time since bore so threatening an aspect, are, it is to be hoped, in a fair train of settlement in a manner just and honorable to both parties.

The isthmus of Central America, including that of Panama, is the great highway between the Atlantic and Pacific over which a large portion of the commerce of the world is destined to pass. The United States are more deeply interested than any other nation in preserving the freedom and security of all the communications across this isthmus. It is our duty, therefore, to take care that they shall not be interrupted either by invasions from our own country or by wars between the independent States of Central America. Under our treaty with New Granada of the 12th December, 1846, we are bound to guarantee the neutrality of the Isthmus of Panama, through which the Panama Railroad passes, "as well as the rights of sovereignty and property which New Granada has and possesses over the said territory." This obligation is rounded upon equivalents granted by the treaty to the Government and people of the United States.

Under these circumstances I recommend to Congress the passage of an act authorizing the President, in case of necessity, to employ the land and naval forces of the United States to carry into effect this guaranty of neutrality and protection. I also recommend similar legislation for the security of any other route across the Isthmus in which we may acquire an interest by treaty.

With the independent Republics on this continent it is both our duty and our interest to cultivate the most friendly relations. We can never feel indifferent to their fate, and must always rejoice in their prosperity. Unfortunately both for them and for us, our example and advice have lost much of their influence in consequence of the lawless expeditions which have been fitted out against some of them within the limits of our country. Nothing is better calculated to retard our steady material progress or impair our character as a nation than the toleration of such enterprises in violation of the law of nations.

It is one of the first and highest duties of any independent state in its relations with the members of the great family of nations to restrain its people from acts of hostile aggression against their citizens or subjects. The most eminent writers on public law do not hesitate to denounce such hostile acts as robbery and murder.

Weak and feeble states like those of Central America may not feel themselves able to assert and vindicate their rights. The case would be far different if expeditions were set on foot within our own territories to make private war against a powerful nation. If such expeditions were fitted out from abroad against any portion of our own country, to burn down our cities, murder and plunder our people, and usurp our Government, we should call any power on earth to the strictest account for not preventing such enormities.

Ever since the Administration of General Washington acts of Congress have been enforced to punish severely the crime of setting on foot a military expedition within the limits of the United States to proceed from thence against a nation or state with whom we are at peace. The present neutrality act of April 20, 1818, is but little more than a collection of preexisting laws. Under this act the President is empowered to employ the land and naval forces and the militia "for the purpose of preventing the carrying on of any such expedition or enterprise from the territories and jurisdiction of the United States," and the collectors of customs are authorized and required to detain any vessel in port when there is reason to believe she is about to take part in such lawless enterprises.

When it was first rendered probable that an attempt would be made to get up another unlawful expedition against Nicaragua, the Secretary of State issued instructions to the marshals and district attorneys, which were directed by the Secretaries of War and the Navy to the appropriate army and navy officers, requiring them to be vigilant and to use their best exertions in carrying into effect the provisions of the act of 1818. Notwithstanding these precautions, the expedition has escaped from our shores. Such enterprises can do no possible good to the country, but have already inflicted much injury both on its interests and its character. They have prevented peaceful emigration from the United States to the States of Central America, which could not fail to prove highly beneficial to all the parties concerned. In a pecuniary point of view alone our citizens have sustained heavy losses from the seizure and closing of the transit route by the San Juan between the two oceans.

The leader of the recent expedition was arrested at New Orleans, but was discharged on giving bail for his appearance in the insufficient sum of $2,000.

I commend the whole subject to the serious attention of Congress, believing that our duty and our interest, as well as our national character, require that we should adopt such measures as will be effectual in restraining our citizens from committing such outrages.

I regret to inform you that the President of Paraguay has refused to ratify the treaty between the United States and that State as amended by the Senate, the signature of which was mentioned in the message of my predecessor to Congress at the opening of its session in December, 1853. The reasons assigned for this refusal will appear in the correspondence herewith submitted.

It being desirable to ascertain the fitness of the river La Plata and its tributaries for navigation by steam, the United States steamer Water Witch was sent thither for that purpose in 1853. This enterprise was successfully carried on until February, 1855, when, whilst in the peaceful prosecution of her voyage up the Parana River, the steamer was fired upon by a Paraguayan fort. The fire was returned, but as the Water Witch was of small force and not designed for offensive operations, she retired from the conflict. The pretext upon which the attack was made was a decree of the President of Paraguay of October, 1854, prohibiting foreign vessels of war from navigating the rivers of that State. As Paraguay, however, was the owner of but one bank of the river of that name, the other belonging to Corientes, a State of the Argentine Confederation, the right of its Government to expect that such a decree would be obeyed can not be acknowledged. But the Water Witch was not, properly speaking, a vessel of war. She was a small steamer engaged in a scientific enterprise intended for the advantage of commercial states generally. Under these circumstances I am constrained to consider the attack upon her as unjustifiable and as calling for satisfaction from the Paraguayan Government.

Citizens of the United States also who were established in business in Paraguay have had their property seized and taken from them, and have otherwise been treated by the authorities in an insulting and arbitrary manner, which requires redress.

A demand for these purposes will be made in a firm but conciliatory spirit. This will the more probably be granted if the Executive shall have authority to use other means in the event of a refusal. This is accordingly recommended.

It is unnecessary to state in detail the alarming condition of the Territory of Kansas at the time of my inauguration. The opposing parties then stood in hostile array against each other, and any accident might have relighted the flames of civil war. Besides, at this critical moment Kansas was left without a governor by the resignation of Governor Geary.

On the 19th of February previous the Territorial legislature had passed a law providing for the election of delegates on the third Monday of June to a convention to meet on the first Monday of September for the purpose of framing a constitution preparatory to admission into the Union. This law was in the main fair and just, and it is to be regretted that all the qualified electors had not registered themselves and voted under its provisions.

At the time of the election for delegates an extensive organization existed in the Territory whose avowed object it was, if need be, to put down the lawful government by force and to establish a government of their own under the so-called Topeka constitution. The persons attached to this revolutionary organization abstained from taking any part in the election.

The act of the Territorial legislature had omitted to provide for submitting to the people the constitution which might be framed by the convention, and in the excited state of public feeling throughout Kansas an apprehension extensively prevailed that a design existed to force upon them a constitution in relation to slavery against their will. In this emergency it became my duty, as it was my unquestionable right, having in view the union of all good citizens in support of the Territorial laws, to express an opinion on the true construction of the provisions concerning slavery contained in the organic act of Congress of the 30th May, 1854. Congress declared it to be "the true intent and meaning of this act not to legislate slavery into any Territory or State, nor to exclude it therefrom, but to leave the people thereof perfectly free to form and regulate their domestic institutions in their own way." Under it Kansas, "when admitted as a State," was to "be received into the Union with or without slavery, as their constitution may prescribe at the time of their admission."

Did Congress mean by this language that the delegates elected to frame a constitution should have authority finally to decide the question of slavery, or did they intend by leaving it to the people that the people of Kansas themselves should decide this question by a direct vote? On this subject I confess I had never entertained a serious doubt, and therefore in my instructions to Governor Walker of the 28th March last I merely said that when "a constitution shall be submitted to the people of the Territory they must be protected in the exercise of their right of voting for or against that instrument, and the fair expression of the popular will must not be interrupted by fraud or violence."

In expressing this opinion it was far from my intention to interfere with the decision of the people of Kansas, either for or against slavery. From this I have always carefully abstained. Intrusted with the duty of taking "care that the laws be faithfully executed," my only desire was that the people of Kansas should furnish to Congress the evidence required by the organic act, whether for or against slavery, and in this manner smooth their passage into the Union. In emerging from the condition of Territorial dependence into that of a sovereign State it was their duty, in my opinion, to make known their will by the votes of the majority on the direct question whether this important domestic institution should or should not continue to exist. Indeed, this was the only possible mode in which their will could be authentically ascertained.

The election of delegates to a convention must necessarily take place in separate districts. From this cause it may readily happen, as has often been the case, that a majority of the people of a State or Territory are on one side of a question, whilst a majority of the representatives from the several districts into which it is divided may be upon the other side. This arises front the fact that in some districts delegates may be elected by small majorities, whilst in others those of different sentiments may receive majorities sufficiently great not only to overcome the votes given for the former, but to leave a large majority of the whole people in direct opposition to a majority of the delegates. Besides, our history proves that influences may be brought to bear on the representative sufficiently powerful to induce him to disregard the will of his constituents. The truth is that no other authentic and satisfactory mode exists of ascertaining the will of a majority of the people of any State or Territory on an important and exciting question like that of slavery in Kansas except by leaving it to a direct vote. How wise, then, was it for Congress to pass over all subordinate and intermediate agencies and proceed directly to the source of all legitimate power under our institutions!

How vain would any other principle prove in practice! This may be illustrated by the case of Kansas. Should she be admitted into the Union with a constitution either maintaining or abolishing slavery against the sentiment of the people, this could have no other effect than to continue and to exasperate the existing agitation during the brief period required to make the constitution conform to the irresistible will of the majority.

The friends and supporters of the Nebraska and Kansas act, when struggling on a recent occasion to sustain its wise provisions before the great tribunal of the American people, never differed about its true meaning on this subject. Everywhere throughout the Union they publicly pledged their faith and their honor that they would cheerfully submit the question of slavery to the decision of the bona fide people of Kansas, without any restriction or qualification whatever. All were cordially united upon the great doctrine of popular sovereignty, which is the vital principle of our free institutions. Had it then been insinuated from any quarter that it would be a sufficient compliance with the requisitions of the organic law for the members of a convention thereafter to be elected to withhold the question of slavery from the people and to substitute their own will for that of a legally ascertained majority of all their constituents, this would have been instantly rejected. Everywhere they remained true to the resolution adopted on a celebrated occasion recognizing "the right of the people of all the Territories, including Kansas and Nebraska, acting through the legally and fairly expressed will of a majority of actual residents, and whenever the number of their inhabitants justifies it, to form a constitution with or without slavery and be admitted into the Union upon terms of perfect equality with the other States."

The convention to frame a constitution for Kansas met on the first Monday of September last. They were called together by virtue of an act of the Territorial legislature, whose lawful existence had been recognized by Congress in different forms and by different enactments. A large proportion of the citizens of Kansas did not think proper to register their names and to vote at the election for delegates; but an opportunity to do this having been fairly afforded, their refusal to avail themselves of their right could in no manner affect the legality of the convention. This convention proceeded to frame a constitution for Kansas, and finally adjourned on the 7th day of November. But little difficulty occurred in the convention except on the subject of slavery. The truth is that the general provisions of our recent State constitutions are so similar and, I may add, so excellent that the difference between them is not essential. Under the earlier practice of the Government no constitution framed by the convention of a Territory preparatory to its admission into the Union as a State had been submitted to the people. I trust, however, the example set by the last Congress, requiring that the constitution of Minnesota "should be subject to the approval and ratification of the people of the proposed State," may be followed on future occasions. I took it for granted that the convention of Kansas would act in accordance with this example, rounded, as it is, on correct principles, and hence my instructions to Governor Walker in favor of submitting the constitution to the people were expressed in general and unqualified terms.

In the Kansas-Nebraska act, however, this requirement, as applicable to the whole constitution, had not been inserted, and the convention were not bound by its terms to submit any other portion of the instrument to an election except that which relates to the "domestic institution" of slavery. This will be rendered clear by a simple reference to its language. It was "not to legislate slavery into any Territory or State, nor to exclude it therefrom, but to leave the people thereof perfectly free to form and regulate their domestic institutions in their own way." According to the plain construction of the sentence, the words "domestic institutions" have a direct, as they have an appropriate, reference to slavery. "Domestic institutions" are limited to the family. The relation between master and slave and a few others are "domestic institutions," and are entirely distinct from institutions of a political character. Besides, there was no question then before

Congress, nor, indeed, has there since been any serious question before the people of Kansas or the country, except that which relates to the "domestic institution" of slavery. The convention, after an angry and excited debate, finally determined, by a majority of only two, to submit the question of slavery to the people, though at the last forty-three of the fifty delegates present affixed their signatures to the constitution.

A large majority of the convention were in favor of establishing slavery in Kansas. They accordingly inserted an article in the constitution for this purpose similar in form to those which had been adopted by other Territorial conventions. In the schedule, however, providing for the transition from a Territorial to a State government the question has been fairly and explicitly referred to the people whether they will have a constitution "with or without slavery." It declares that before the constitution adopted by the convention "shall be sent to Congress for admission into the Union as a State" an election shall be held to decide this question, at which all the white male inhabitants of the Territory above the age of 21 are entitled to vote. They are to vote by ballot, and "the ballots cast at said election shall be indorsed 'constitution with slavery' and 'constitution with no slavery.'" If there be a majority in favor of the "constitution with slavery," then it is to be transmitted to Congress by the president of the convention in its original form; if, on the contrary, there shall be a majority in favor of the "constitution with no slavery," "then the article providing for slavery shall be stricken from the constitution by the president of this convention;" and it is expressly declared that "no slavery shall exist in the State of Kansas, except that the right of property in slaves now in the Territory shall in no manner be interfered with;" and in that event it is made his duty to have the constitution thus ratified transmitted to the Congress of the United States for the admission of the State into the Union.

At this election every citizen will have an opportunity of expressing his opinion by his vote "whether Kansas shall be received into the Union with or without slavery," and thus this exciting question may be peacefully settled in the very mode required by the organic law. The election will be held under legitimate authority, and if any portion of the inhabitants shall refuse to vote, a fair opportunity to do so having been presented, this will be their own voluntary act and they alone will be responsible for the consequences.

Whether Kansas shall be a free or a slave State must eventually, under some authority, be decided by an election; and the question can never be more clearly or distinctly presented to the people than it is at the present moment. Should this opportunity be rejected she may be involved for years in domestic discord, and possibly in civil war, before she can again make up the issue now so fortunately tendered and again reach the point she has already attained.

Kansas has for some years occupied too much of the public attention. It is high time this should be directed to far more important objects. When once admitted into the Union, whether with or without slavery, the excitement beyond her own limits will speedily pass away, and she will then for the first time be left, as she ought to have been long since, to manage her own affairs in her own way. If her constitution on the subject of slavery or on any other subject be displeasing to a majority of the people, no human power can prevent them from changing it within a brief period. Under these circumstances it may well be questioned whether the peace and quiet of the whole country are not of greater importance than the mere temporary triumph of either of the political parties in Kansas.

Should the constitution without slavery be adopted by the votes of the majority, the rights of property in slaves now in the Territory are reserved. The number of these is very small, but if it were greater the provision would be equally just and reasonable. The slaves were brought into the Territory under the Constitution of the United States and are now the property of their masters. This point has at length been finally decided by the highest judicial tribunal of the country, and this upon the plain principle that when a confederacy of sovereign States acquire a new territory at their joint expense both equality and justice demand that the citizens of one and all of them shall have the right to take into it whatsoever is recognized as property by the common Constitution. To have summarily confiscated the property in slaves already in the Territory would have been an act of gross injustice and contrary to the practice of the older States of the Union which have abolished slavery.

A Territorial government was established for Utah by act of Congress approved the 9th September, 1850, and the Constitution and laws of the United States were thereby extended over it "so far as the same or any provisions thereof may be applicable." This act provided for the appointment by the President, by and with the advice and consent of the Senate, of a governor (who was to be ex officio superintendent of Indian affairs), a secretary, three judges of the supreme court, a marshal, and a district attorney. Subsequent acts provided for the appointment of the officers necessary to extend our land and our Indian system over the Territory. Brigham Young was appointed the first governor on the 20th September, 1850, and has held the office ever since. Whilst Governor Young has been both governor and superintendent of Indian affairs throughout this period, he has been at the same time the head of the church called the Latter-day Saints, and professes to govern its members and dispose of their property by direct inspiration and authority from the Almighty. His power has been, therefore, absolute over both church and state.

The people of Utah almost exclusively belong to this church, and believing with a fanatical spirit that he is governor of the Territory by divine appointment, they obey his commands as if these were direct revelations from Heaven. If, therefore, he chooses that his government shall come into collision with the Government of the United States, the members of the Mormon Church will yield implicit obedience to his will. Unfortunately, existing facts leave but little doubt that such is his determination. Without entering upon a minute history of occurrences, it is sufficient to say that all the officers of the United States, judicial and executive, with the single exception of two Indian agents, have found it necessary for their own personal safety to withdraw from the Territory, and there no longer remains any government in Utah but the despotism of Brigham Young. This being the condition of affairs in the Territory, I could not mistake the path of duty. As Chief Executive Magistrate I was bound to restore the supremacy of the Constitution and laws within its limits. In order to effect this purpose, I appointed a new governor and other Federal officers for Utah and sent with them a military force for their protection and to aid as a posse comitatus in case of need in the execution of the laws.

With the religious opinions of the Mormons, as long as they remained mere opinions, however deplorable in themselves and revolting to the moral and religious sentiments of all Christendom, I had no right to interfere. Actions alone, when in violation of the Constitution and laws of the United States, become the legitimate subjects for the jurisdiction of the civil magistrate. My instructions to Governor Cumming have therefore been framed in strict accordance with these principles. At their date a hope was indulged that no necessity might exist for employing the military in restoring and maintaining the authority of the law, but this hope has now vanished. Governor Young has by proclamation declared his determination to maintain his power by force, and has already committed acts of hostility against the United States. Unless he should retrace his steps the Territory of Utah will be in a state of open rebellion. He has committed these acts of hostility notwithstanding Major Van Vliet, an officer of the Army, sent to Utah by the Commanding General to purchase provisions for the troops, had given him the strongest assurances of the peaceful intentions of the Government, and that the troops would only be employed as a posse comitatus when called on by the civil authority to aid in the execution of the laws.

There is reason to believe that Governor Young has long contemplated this result. He knows that the continuance of his despotic power depends upon the exclusion of all settlers from the Territory except those who will acknowledge his divine mission and implicitly obey his will, and that an enlightened public opinion there would soon prostrate institutions at war with the laws both of God and man. "He has therefore for several years, in order to maintain his independence, been industriously employed in collecting and fabricating arms and munitions of war and in disciplining the Mormons for military service." As superintendent of Indian affairs he has had an opportunity of tampering with the Indian tribes and exciting their hostile feelings against the United States. This, according to our information, he has accomplished in regard to some of these tribes, while others have remained true to their allegiance and have communicated his intrigues to our Indian agents. He has laid in a store of provisions for three years, which in case of necessity, as he informed Major Van Vliet, he will conceal, "and then take to the mountains and bid defiance to all the powers of the Government."

A great part of all this may be idle boasting, but yet no wise government will lightly estimate the efforts which may be inspired by such frenzied fanaticism as exists among the Mormons in Utah. This is the first rebellion which has existed in our Territories, and humanity itself requires that we should put it down in such a manner that it shall be the last. To trifle with it would be to encourage it and to render it formidable. We ought to go there with such an imposing force as to convince these deluded people that resistance would be vain, and thus spare the effusion of blood. We can in this manner best convince them that we are their friends, not their enemies. In order to accomplish this object it will be necessary, according to the estimate of the War Department, to raise four additional regiments; and this I earnestly recommend to Congress. At the present moment of depression in the revenues of the country I am sorry to be obliged to recommend such a measure; but I feel confident of the support of Congress, cost what it may, in suppressing the insurrection and in restoring and maintaining the sovereignty of the Constitution and laws over the Territory of Utah.

I recommend to Congress the establishment of a Territorial government over Arizona, incorporating with it such portions of New Mexico as they may deem expedient. I need scarcely adduce arguments in support of this recommendation. We are bound to protect the lives and the property of our citizens inhabiting Arizona, and these are now without any efficient protection. Their present number is already considerable, and is rapidly increasing, notwithstanding the disadvantages under which they labor. Besides, the proposed Territory is believed to be rich in mineral and agricultural resources, especially in silver and copper. The mails of the United States to California are now carried over it throughout its whole extent, and this route is known to be the nearest and believed to be the best to the Pacific.

Long experience has deeply convinced me that a strict construction of the powers granted to Congress is the only true, as well as the only safe, theory of the Constitution. Whilst this principle shall guide my public conduct, I consider it clear that under the war-making power Congress may appropriate money for the Construction of a military road through the

Territories of the United States when this is absolutely necessary for the defense of any of the States against foreign invasion. The Constitution has conferred upon Congress power "to declare war," "to raise and support armies," "to provide and maintain a navy," and to call forth the militia to "repel invasions." These high sovereign powers necessarily involve important and responsible public duties, and among them there is none so sacred and so imperative as that of preserving our soil from the invasion of a foreign enemy. The Constitution has therefore left nothing on this point to construction, but expressly requires that "the United States shall protect each of them [the States] against invasion." Now if a military road over our own Territories be indispensably necessary to enable us to meet and repel the invader, it follows as a necessary consequence not only that we possess the power, but it is our imperative duty to construct such a road. It would be an absurdity to invest a government with the unlimited power to make and conduct war and at the same time deny to it the only means of reaching and defeating the enemy at the frontier. Without such a road it is quite evident we can not "protect" California and our Pacific possessions "against invasion." We can not by any other means transport men and munitions of war from the Atlantic States in sufficient time successfully to defend these remote and distant portions of the Republic.

Experience has proved that the routes across the isthmus of Central America are at best but a very uncertain and unreliable mode of communication. But even if this were not the case, they would at once be closed against us in the event of war with a naval power so much stronger than our own as to enable it to blockade the ports at either end of these routes. After all, therefore, we can only rely upon a military road through our own Territories; and ever since the origin of the Government Congress has been in the practice of appropriating money from the public Treasury for the construction of such roads.

The difficulties and the expense of constructing a military railroad to connect our Atlantic and Pacific States have been greatly exaggerated. The distance on the Arizona route, near the thirty-second parallel of north latitude, between the western boundary of Texas, on the Rio Grande, and the eastern boundary of California, on the Colorado, from the best explorations now within our knowledge, does not exceed 470 miles, and the face of the country is in the main favorable. For obvious reasons the Government ought not to undertake the work itself by means of its own agents. This ought to be committed to other agencies, which Congress might assist, either by grants of land or money, or by both, upon such terms and conditions as they may deem most beneficial for the country. Provision might thus be made not only for the safe, rapid, and economical transportation of troops and munitions of war, but also of the public mails. The commercial interests of the whole country, both East and West, would be greatly promoted by such a road, and, above all, it would be a powerful additional bond of union. And although advantages of this kind, whether postal, commercial, or political, can not confer constitutional power, yet they may furnish auxiliary arguments in favor of expediting a work which, in my judgment, is clearly embraced within the war-making power.

For these reasons I commend to the friendly consideration of Congress the subject of the Pacific Railroad, without finally committing myself to any particular route.

The report of the Secretary of the Treasury will furnish a detailed statement of the condition of the public finances and of the respective branches of the public service devolved upon that Department of the Government. By this report it appears that the amount of revenue received from all sources into the Treasury during the fiscal year ending the 30th June, 1857, was $68,631,513.67, which amount, with the balance of $19,901,325.45 remaining in the Treasury at the commencement of the year, made an aggregate for the service of the year of $88,532,839.12.

The public expenditures for the fiscal year ending 30th June, 1857, amounted to $70,822,724.85, of which $5,943,896.91 were applied to the redemption of the public debt, including interest and premium, leaving in the Treasury at the commencement of the present fiscal year, on the 1st July, 1857, $17,710,114.27.

The receipts into the Treasury for the first quarter of the present fiscal year, commencing 1st July, 1857, were $20,929,819.81, and the estimated receipts of the remaining three quarters to the 30th June, 1858, are $36,750,000, making, with the balance before stated, an aggregate of $75,389,934.08 for the service of the present fiscal year.

The actual expenditures during the first quarter of the present fiscal year were $23,714,528.37, of which $3,895,232.39 were applied to the redemption of the public debt, including interest and premium. The probable expenditures of the remaining three quarters to 30th June, 1858, are $51,248,530.04, including interest on the public debt, making an aggregate of $74,963,058.41, leaving an estimated balance in the Treasury at the close of the present fiscal year of $426,875.67.

The amount of the public debt at the commencement of the present fiscal year was $29,060,386.90.

The amount redeemed since the 1st of July was $3,895,232.39, leaving a balance unredeemed at this time of $25,165,154.51.

The amount of estimated expenditures for the remaining three quarters of the present fiscal year will in all probability be increased from the causes set forth in the report of the Secretary. His suggestion, therefore, that authority should be given to supply any temporary deficiency by the issue of a limited amount of Treasury notes is approved, and I accordingly recommend the passage of such a law.

As stated in the report of the Secretary, the tariff of March 3, 1857, has been in operation for so short a period of time and under circumstances so unfavorable to a just development of its results as a revenue measure that I should regard it as inexpedient, at least for the present, to undertake its revision.

I transmit herewith the reports made to me by the Secretaries of War and of the Navy, of the Interior, and of the Postmaster-General. They all contain valuable and important information and suggestions, which I commend to the favorable consideration of Congress.

I have already recommended the raising of four additional regiments, and the report of the Secretary of War presents strong reasons proving this increase of the Army under existing circumstances to be indispensable.

I would call the special attention of Congress to the recommendation of the Secretary of the Navy in favor of the construction of ten small war steamers of light draft. For some years the Government has been obliged on many occasions to hire such steamers from individuals to supply its pressing wants. At the present moment we have no armed vessel in the Navy which can penetrate the rivers of China. We have but few which can enter any of the harbors south of Norfolk, although many millions of foreign and domestic commerce annually pass in and out of these harbors. Some of our most valuable interests and most vulnerable points are thus left exposed. This class of vessels of light draft, great speed, and heavy guns would be formidable in coast defense. The cost of their construction will not be great and they will require but a comparatively small expenditure to keep them in commission. In time of peace they will prove as effective as much larger vessels and more useful. One of them should be at every station where we maintain a squadron, and three or four should be constantly employed on our Atlantic and Pacific coasts. Economy, utility, and efficiency combine to recommend them as almost indispensable. Ten of these small vessels would be of incalculable advantage to the naval service, and the whole cost of their construction would not exceed $2,300,000, or $230,000 each.

The report of the Secretary of the Interior is worthy of grave consideration. It treats of the numerous important and diversified branches of domestic administration intrusted to him by law. Among these the most prominent are the public lands and our relations with the Indians. Our system for the disposal of the public lands, originating with the fathers of the Republic, has been improved as experience pointed the way, and gradually adapted to the growth and settlement of our Western States and Territories. It has worked well in practice. Already thirteen States and seven Territories have been carved out of these lands, and still more than a thousand millions of acres remain unsold. What a boundless prospect this presents to our country of future prosperity and power!

We have heretofore disposed of 363,862,464 acres of the public land.

Whilst the public lands, as a source of revenue, are of great importance, their importance is far greater as furnishing homes for a hardy and independent race of honest and industrious citizens who desire to subdue and cultivate the soil. They ought to be administered mainly with a view of promoting this wise and benevolent policy. In appropriating them for any other purpose we ought to use even greater economy than if they had been converted into money and the proceeds were already in the public Treasury. To squander away this richest and noblest inheritance which any people have ever enjoyed upon objects of doubtful constitutionality or expediency would be to violate one of the most important trusts ever committed to any people. Whilst I do not deny to Congress the power, when acting bona fide as a proprietor, to give away portions of them for the purpose of increasing the value of the remainder, yet, considering the great temptation to abuse this power, we can not be too cautious in its exercise. Actual settlers under existing laws are protected against other purchasers at the public sales in their right of preemption to the extent of a quarter section, or 160 acres, of land. The remainder may then be disposed of at public or entered at private sale in unlimited quantities. Speculation has of late years prevailed to a great extent in the public lands. The consequence has been that large portions of them have become the property of individuals and companies, and thus the price is greatly enhanced to those who desire to purchase for actual settlement. In order to limit the area of speculation as much as possible, the extinction of the Indian title and the extension of the public surveys ought only to keep pace with the tide of emigration.

If Congress should hereafter grant alternate sections to States or companies, as they have done heretofore, I recommend that the intermediate sections retained by the Government should be subject to preemption by actual settlers.

It ought ever to be our cardinal policy to reserve the public lands as much as may be for actual settlers, and this at moderate prices. We shall thus not only best promote the prosperity of the new States and Territories and the power of the Union, but shall secure homes for our posterity for many generations.

The extension of our limits has brought within our jurisdiction many additional and populous tribes of Indians, a large proportion of which are wild, untractable, and difficult to control. Predatory and warlike in their disposition and habits, it is impossible altogether to restrain them from committing aggressions on each other, as well as upon our frontier citizens and those emigrating to our distant States and Territories. Hence expensive military expeditions are frequently necessary to overawe and chastise the more lawless and hostile. The present system of making them valuable presents to influence them to remain at peace has proved ineffectual. It is believed to be the better policy to colonize them in suitable localities where they can receive the rudiments of education and be gradually induced to adopt habits of industry. So far as the experiment has been tried it has worked well in practice, and it will doubtless prove to be less expensive than the present system.

The whole number of Indians within our territorial limits is believed to be, from the best data in the Interior Department, about 325,000. The tribes of Cherokees, Choctaws, Chickasaws, and Creeks settled in the Territory set apart for them west of Arkansas are rapidly advancing in education and in all the arts of civilization and self-government and we may indulge the agreeable anticipation that at no very distant day they will be incorporated into the Union as one of the sovereign States.

It will be seen from the report of the Postmaster-General that the Post-Office Department still continues to depend on the Treasury, as it has been compelled to do for several years past, for an important portion of the means of sustaining and extending its operations. Their rapid growth and expansion are shown by a decennial statement of the number of post-offices and the length of post-roads, commencing with the year 1827. In that year there were 7,000 post-offices; in 1837, 11,177; in 1847, 15,146, and in 1857 they number 26,586. In this year 1,725 post-offices have been established and 704 discontinued, leaving a net increase of 1,021. The postmasters of 368 offices are appointed by the President.

The length of post-roads in 1827 was 105,336 miles; in 1837,141,242 miles; in 1847, 153,818 miles, and in the year 1857 there are 242,601 miles of post-road, including 22,530 miles of railroad on which the mails are transported.

The expenditures of the Department for the fiscal year ending on the 30th June, 1857, as adjusted by the Auditor, amounted to $11,507,670. To defray these expenditures there was to the credit of the Department on the 1st July, 1856, the sum of $789,599; the gross revenue of the year, including the annual allowances for the transportation of free mail matter, produced $8,053,951, and the remainder was supplied by the appropriation from the Treasury of $2,250,000 granted by the act of Congress approved August 18, 1856, and by the appropriation of $666,883 made by the act of March 3, 1857, leaving $252,763 to be carried to the credit of the Department in the accounts of the current year. I commend to your consideration the report of the Department in relation to the establishment of the overland mail route from the Mississippi River to San Francisco, Cal. The route was selected with my full concurrence, as the one, in my judgment, best calculated to attain the important objects contemplated by Congress.

The late disastrous monetary revulsion may have one good effect should it cause both the Government and the people to return to the practice of a wise and judicious economy both in public and private expenditures.

An overflowing Treasury has led to habits of prodigality and extravagance in our legislation. It has induced Congress to make large appropriations to objects for which they never would have provided had it been necessary to raise the amount of revenue required to meet them by increased taxation or by loans. We are now compelled to pause in our career and to scrutinize our expenditures with the utmost vigilance; and in performing this duty I pledge my cooperation to the extent of my constitutional competency.

It ought to be observed at the same time that true public economy does not consist in withholding the means necessary to accomplish important national objects intrusted to us by the Constitution, and especially such as may be necessary for the common defense. In the present crisis of the country it is our duty to confine our appropriations to objects of this character, unless in cases where justice to individuals may demand a different course. In all cases care ought to be taken that the money granted by Congress shall be faithfully and economically applied.

Under the Federal Constitution "every bill which shall have passed the House of Representatives and the Senate shall, before it become a law," be approved and signed by the President; and if not approved, "he shall return it with his objections to that House in which it shall have originated." In order to perform this high and responsible duty, sufficient time must be allowed the President to read and examine every bill presented to him for approval. Unless this be afforded, the Constitution becomes a dead letter in this particular, and; even worse, it becomes a means of deception. Our constituents, seeing the President's approval and signature attached to each act of Congress, are induced to believe that he has actually performed his duty, when in truth nothing is in many cases more unfounded.

From the practice of Congress such an examination of each bill as the Constitution requires has been rendered impossible. The most important business of each session is generally crowded into its last hours, and the alternative presented to the President is either to violate the constitutional duty which he owes to the people and approve bills which for want of time it is impossible he should have examined, or by his refusal to do this subject the country and individuals to great loss and inconvenience.

Besides, a practice has grown up of late years to legislate in appropriation bills at the last hours of the session on new and important subjects. This practice constrains the President either to suffer measures to become laws which he does not approve or to incur the risk of stopping the wheels of the Government by vetoing an appropriation bill. Formerly such bills were confined to specific appropriations for carrying into effect existing laws and the well-established policy of the country, and little time was then requited by the President for their examination.

For my own part, I have deliberately determined that I shall approve no bills which I have not examined, and it will be a case of extreme and most urgent necessity which shall ever induce me to depart from this rule. I therefore respectfully but earnestly recommend that the two Houses would allow the President at least two days previous to the adjournment of each session within which no new bill shall be presented to him for approval. Under the existing joint rule one day is allowed, but this rule has been hitherto so constantly suspended in practice that important bills continue to be presented to him up till the very last moments of the session. In a large majority of cases no great public inconvenience can arise from the want of time to examine their provisions, because the Constitution has declared that if a bill be presented to the President within the last ten days of the session he is not required to return it, either with an approval or with a veto, "in which case it shall not be a law." It may then lie over and be taken up and passed at the next session. Great inconvenience would only be experienced in regard to appropriation bills, but, fortunately, under the late excellent law allowing a salary instead of a per diem to members of Congress the expense and inconvenience of a called session will be greatly reduced.

I can not conclude without commending to your favorable consideration the interest of the people of this District. Without a representative on the floor of Congress, they have for this very reason peculiar claims upon our just regard. To this I know, from my long acquaintance with them, they are eminently entitled.